"Just Look Inside". This writing journal consist of 30 inspirational sayings, written by me, and supported by scripture.

It is my hope that this journal will help you see that we each have gifts that lie within us. As we all experience different seasons in life, what better way to express them than to journal your individual journey.

Thank You,
Janice

Faith is the name of life's race, so use it to your advantage.

Romans 1:17 For in it the righteousness of God is revealed from faith to faith; as it is written, "The just shall live by faith."

Remember that God's blessings are true and unchangeable.

Malachi 3:6 I the LORD do not change

_____

_____

_____

_____

_____

_____

_____

_____

_____

_____

_____

_____

_____

_____

_____

_____

_____

_____

_____

_____

_____

_____

_____

Hope is wanting something to happen, knowing is believing that it will.

Matthew 21:22 And all things, whatsoever ye shall ask in prayer, believing, ye shall receive.

_____

_____

_____

_____

_____

_____

_____

_____

_____

_____

_____

_____

_____

_____

_____

_____

_____

_____

_____

_____

_____

_____

_____

Loving someone completely means loving them no matter their state of being.

1 John 3:16 This is how we know what love is: Jesus Christ laid down his life for us. And we ought to lay down our lives for our brothers and sisters.

Be sure that the words that flow through you only bring life to others.

Romans 14:19 Therefore let us pursue the things which make for peace and the things by which one may edify another.

Nothing and no one can keep you in bondage unless you allow them.

John 8:36 - Therefore if the son makes you free, you shall be free indeed

Don't walk away from yourself; stay faithful to your calling.

Job 40:10 Then adorn yourself with majesty and splendor, and array yourself with glory and beauty.

Never place unrealistic expectations on someone just to have your way. This will only lead to disappointment.

If you live your life in fragments, it will never be complete.

Eph 6:13 Therefore take up the whole armor of God, that you may be able to withstand in the evil day, and having done all, to stand

Even if your pace changes, stay in the race.

1 Corinthian's 9:24 Do you not know that those who run in a race all run, but one receives the prize? Run in such a way that you may obtain it.

_____

_____

_____

_____

_____

_____

_____

_____

_____

_____

_____

_____

_____

_____

_____

_____

_____

_____

_____

_____

_____

_____

No storm in life can disturb the peace God has given us. Remember you can speak to the mountain.

Psalm 91:10 No harm will overtake you, no disaster will come near you.

Dare to trust God and let peace overtake you!.

Isaiah 40:31 But those who wait on the Lord Shall renew their strength; They shall mount up with wings like eagles, they shall run and not be weary, they shall walk and not faint.

_____
_____
_____
_____
_____
_____
_____
_____
_____
_____
_____
_____
_____
_____
_____
_____
_____
_____
_____
_____
_____
_____
_____
_____

Always think of things that bring you peace and speak those things that bring joy to your life.

Proverbs 23:7 For as he thinks in his heart, so is he

_____

_____

_____

_____

_____

_____

_____

_____

_____

_____

_____

_____

_____

_____

_____

_____

_____

_____

_____

_____

_____

_____

_____

Reflecting on your past has only equipped you for the future you desire to have. Life is full of lessons, use them wisely.

Walking in the wisdom of the world will only lead to destruction. Walking in the wisdom of the word always bring life's blessings.

Psalms 15:2 - He that walketh uprightly, and worketh righteousness, and speaks the truth in his heart.

No man knows your heart, only God.

Luke 16:15 He said to them, "You are the ones who justify yourselves in the eyes of others, but God knows your hearts. What people value highly is detestable in God's sight.

We are pardoned from all the wrong we have done. If you
don't believe me, just look at the cross.

*Romans 4:7 Blessed are those whose lawless deeds are forgiven, and whose
sins are covered.*

_____

_____

_____

_____

_____

_____

_____

_____

_____

_____

_____

_____

_____

_____

_____

_____

_____

_____

_____

_____

_____

_____

_____

True love is a spiritual energy that can only be generated by its source, God himself.

1 John 4:7 7 Beloved, let us love one another, for love is of God; and everyone who loves is born of God and knows God.

We must remind ourselves that the paths we take should be directed by God himself. If we get off track, he is always there to put us back in line.

Psalm 23:3 He restores my soul; He leads me in the paths of righteousness For His name's sake.

There comes a time in your life when stillness is all you need.

Psalm 46:10 Be still and know that I am God, I will be exalted among the nations and I will be exalted in the earth!

_____

_____

_____

_____

_____

_____

_____

_____

_____

_____

_____

_____

_____

_____

_____

_____

_____

_____

_____

_____

_____

_____

_____

_____

_____

Remember each day that you are alive, you have the unique ability to tell your own story to change the world around you. What will history say about you?

Matthew 5:16 Let your light so shine before men, that they may see your good works and glorify your Father in heaven.

Only trust what the father has promised to you and allow this to be the anchor of your soul.

Deuteronomy 26:17 Today you have proclaimed the Lord to be your God, and that you will walk in His ways and keep His statutes, His commandments, and His judgments, and that you will obey His voice

Never drink water from a dripping faucet as it only wets your pallet, but it does not quench your thirst.

Jeremiah 2:13 For my people have committed two evils: they have forsaken me, the fountain of living waters, and hewed out cisterns for themselves, broken cisterns that can hold no water.

Regardless of where you may be in life, take time throughout the day to stop and meditate on something that will make you smile.

How you treat your neighbor is a reflection of how you see yourself.

Matthew 22:39 And the second is like it: 'You shall love your neighbor as yourself.'

No wall, no door, no person, can keep you in bondage. You have the power within yourself to move all obstacles. There is forever greatness in you.

In order to make a change you must first change what is in your heart, and your actions will follow.

You are destined for a great purpose. Don't allow the issues of life shortcut you from fulfilling your story.

You need to know that there are still miracles that have your name on it.

My relationship with God is reflected in the way I treat others.

John 13:34-35 "A new command I give you: Love one another. As I have loved you, so you must love one another. By this everyone will know that you are my disciples if you love one another."

*This Journal is dedicated to my
children Joi, Janaiah & Jesse who
continue to encourage me.
In loving memory of my parents
Lovell and Patsy Day.*

Made in the USA
San Bernardino, CA
09 August 2020

76742507R00063